CW00921243

Created and published by Knock Knock
Distributed by Who's There, Inc.
Venice, CA 90291
knockknockstuff.com

ISBN: 978-160106059-4
UPC: 825703-50109-4

25 24 23 22 21 20

Contents

"I must be dancing with the devil,
because you're hot as hell."

Introduction

Paralyzed by a fear of rejection? Unable to muster the courage to walk across a room and introduce yourself? Don't worry—it's not you, it's your words. Specifically, the words you lack. With the right lines, however, you'll suddenly find yourself emboldened to go where you've avoided thus far—straight up to the object of your desire.

Singles are everywhere—to be precise, there are 95.7 million of them in the United States, 43 percent of all citizens over the age of fifteen. Of these, 63 percent have never been married, 23 percent are divorced, and 14 percent are widowed. As evidence of this desire to mate, Internet dating has exploded. According to *Online Dating Magazine*, 40 million Americans use online dating services. Despite the advent of Web love, however, there are still individuals who like to do things the old-fashioned way: face to face. According to a poll conducted by TopDatingTips.com, the breakdown for the top-ten places to meet a romantic partner are as follows: at work (22 percent), at a bar (18 percent), on the Internet (18 percent), at a club (11 percent), while playing a sport (7 percent), at the beach (4 percent), at the mall (4 percent), at a social club (4 percent), at church (2 percent), and other (9 percent; it's not clear what happened to the other 1 percent). While online dating ranks high, a full 82 percent of the locations are live and in person—which means you need a good arsenal of pickup lines and come-ons, not just a composed bit of email wit.

Also according to TopDatingTips. com, 42 percent of respondents characterize meeting new people as "quite difficult," while another 20 percent claim it's "very difficult" or "impossible." Given the number of singles, this clearly isn't due to a lack of warm bodies, and it's a well-known fact that everyone is looking for love—or at least a hookup. One can only assume that people lack the words—and therefore the courage—to make the first move.

Fortunately, *Pickups and Come-Ons for All Occasions* gives you the tools to cruise. Whether you study in advance or carry the pocket-sized volume for reference, you'll never again be at a loss for overture verbiage. Life is getting increasingly complex and demanding, and few of us have time to come up with our own powerful pickups, so we've done the work for you.

Some of these lines are tried-and-true while others are off-the-wall. You can choose the classic approach, flattery, in "All About You," or you can toot your own horn in "All About Me." With "Context-Specific" and "People-Specific," you'll learn how to incorporate situation into your moves. In "Coitus Seeking," you'll get down to brass tacks—or something like that—stating exactly what you're thinking. Finally, in "Famous Flirtations," documented examples of sweet-talking provide inspiration or the opportunity for social plagiarism.

As you learn to use these lines, you'll no doubt face some rejection. However, the law of averages is in your favor. If at first a line doesn't succeed, then try, try again. One of these lines somewhere, sometime, will prevail. Positive thoughts create positive outcomes, while stinking thinking does just the opposite. Having *Pickups and Come-Ons* in your pocket or purse will not only prepare you for any romance-seeking situation, it will give you the confidence you need to conduct yourself enthusiastically in any kind of introductory endeavor.

ALL ABOUT YOU

When flattery will get you everywhere

"WOW, YOU LOOK GREAT!" DOESN'T that feel good? Exactly! Such is the simple art of the compliment. With a little more thought and wit—and a lot more of this book— you'll be turning the compliment into a pickup device in no time.

Focusing on others is one of the surest ways to win their attention and interest. Start slowly,

Tip: Target Insecurities

Most people are insecure about at least one of their physical attributes. You'll gain more points if you compliment one of the areas ranked as those most detested.

Women	Men
1. Stomach	1. Stomach
2. Weight	2. Weight
3. Hips and thighs	3. Muscle tone
4. Buttocks	4. Overall appearance
5. Breasts	5. Chest

flattering someone's overall appearance. Or you can focus on particular features: "great eyes" or "nice smile." Depending on your intentions, you could make your desires clear with a sexual compliment—think curves and legs, abs and ass. The goal is to make your targets feel good about themselves, so good that they'll be willing to talk to you—or more.

Other approaches include corny compliments—saccharine-sweet sentiments sure to make the object of your attraction laugh and melt into your arms. Use sparingly and with humor to avoid the adverse gag and flee reaction.

If charm isn't your thing, however, you could try the more risky insult technique. Although it sounds counterintuitive, there is a growing movement among pickup artists who claim that this strategy, called "negging," works—although you have to wonder about the end result.

So take the first step: a little compliment, or perhaps even a disparaging neg, can go a long way, and as a beginning romancer, you don't have much to lose.

Broke the Mold

Is it a burden being that beautiful?

———◦•◦———

You should be a model. Seriously.

———◦•◦———

I just had to reach out and touch
you—you look too good to be true.

———◦•◦———

Have you always been this cute,
or did you have to practice?

———◦•◦———

Nice to meet you. I'm Cindy,
and you are . . . gorgeous.

———◦•◦———

What does it feel like to be the most
attractive person in this room?

———◦•◦———

When God made you,
she was showing off.

———◦•◦———

If beauty were time, you'd be eternity.

Clearly all the other women
are just rough drafts—because
you're the final copy.

———•—•———

It's a felony in this state to look
that good, but if you go out with
me, I'll let you off with a warning.

———•—•———

If you could put a price tag on
beauty, you'd need to be driven
around in an armored truck.

———•—•———

I've had a terrible day,
and it always makes me feel
better to see a gorgeous woman
smile. Would you smile for me?

———•—•———

I've had an atrocious day, and it always
makes me feel better to see a hot man's
ass. Would you bend over for me?

———•—•———

Did the sun come out, or did
you just smile at me?

You really shouldn't
wear makeup. It's messing
with perfection.

I'd use a line on you,
but I'm too intimidated
by your beauty.

Something's wrong with my eyes—
I can't take them off you.

If I had a nickel for every time
I saw someone as beautiful as
you, I'd have five cents.

Hubba Hubba

Apart from being sexy, what
do you do for a living?

Damn, girl, you have more
curves than a racetrack.

Damn, boy, is that a twelve-pack?

Baby, I've got the fries to
go with that shake.

Just where exactly do those
legs of yours end?

I don't care whether they're real—
they're magnificent.

Ugly Men Rock

Don't hesitate to pick up on beautiful women if
you lack in looks or money. The hotties flock to
the notties thanks in part to genetic percent-
ages. There are simply more stunning women
than handsome men. A study in the *Journal
of Theoretical Biology* submits that attractive
parents are 36 percent more likely to give birth
to girls, statistically increasing the number of
beautiful women. Step up to the plate, gentle-
men—no woman is out of your league.

Your father must have
been a mailman, because
you've got a great package.

———•———

Your father must have
been a mechanic, because
your body is finely tuned.

———•———

Your father must have
been a farmer, because you've
grown some nice melons.

———•———

If it weren't for that damn sun, you'd
be the hottest thing ever created.

———•———

As hot as you are, you must be
contributing to global warming.

———•———

I must have a light switch on my
forehead, because you turn me on.

———•———

I want to wash my laundry on your abs.

I'm sorry to tell you that you're going to hell, because it's a sin to look that good.

———•—•———

Is that a fox on your shoulder,
or am I seeing double?

———•—•———

If I were a pirate, you would be my booty.

———•—•———

Stop, drop, and roll, baby—
you are on *fire*.

———•—•———

You make me want to get a job.

Corn Syrup

You're like a dictionary—
you add meaning to my life.

———•—•———

If I could rearrange the alphabet,
I'd put U and I together.

———•—•———

Come live in my heart and pay no rent.

Nice Guys Finish First

A 2008 Harvard study has proven that being nice works. Playing the classic theoretical game prisoner's dilemma, in which each move invites players to cooperate or defect (punish), subjects who played in a more punishing fashion ended up with less money than those who cooperated. The study's author will next look not at students but at chief executives, but in the meantime, go ahead and assume that being nice in the dating world is a good thing.

Are you from Tennessee?
Because you're the only ten I see.

Would you caress me so I can tell my friends I've been touched by an angel?

How was heaven when you left it?

See these keys? I wish I had the one to your heart.

Quick, somebody call the cops—
you just stole my heart.

———•———

I hope you know CPR, because
you take my breath away.

———•———

I hope you have a map, because
I keep getting lost in your eyes.

———•———

You must be tired,
because you've been running
through my mind all day.

———•———

I'm an artist, and I think
I just found my muse.

———•———

You just made being an artist
harder, because I will never create
something as beautiful as you.

———•———

I never had a dream come
true until today.

How did you guess?
Sweetness is my weakness.

———•◦•———

Your eyes are bluer than the
ocean, and baby, I'm lost at sea.

———•◦•———

I don't know you,
but I think I love you.

———•◦•———

You look like the type of woman
who's heard every line in the
book, so what's one more?

———•◦•———

Way to go, God!

Casting Barbs

Can I buy you a drink, or do
you just want the money?

———•◦•———

If you're going to regret this in the
morning, we can sleep past noon.

Frankly, I don't like a challenge,
which is why I'm talking to you.

———•+•———

Didn't I see you on *Cops*?

———•+•———

Good thing I forgot to wear my contacts.

———•+•———

I'm ugly, you're ugly—it's perfect!

———•+•———

Hi. Can I domesticate you?

———•+•———

Hi. I've been sent to talk to you so
my friend can pick up your friend.

———•+•———

Hi. You'll do.

———•+•———

I don't care much about looks.

———•+•———

I know a great way you can
lose some weight.

I may not be the best-looking woman
here, but who are you to be picky?

———— ◆ ————

I sacrificed my dignity to
come talk to you. The least
you could do is say yes.

———— ◆ ————

I thought I'd come over and give
your self-esteem a boost.

———— ◆ ————

I'm a sweet guy, and you clearly
have a taste for sweets.

———— ◆ ————

I'm feeling charitable. Wanna
go out sometime?

———— ◆ ————

It's your lucky day—I'm on the
rebound, and my standards are low.

———— ◆ ————

You looked better from across
the room, but now that I'm here
I might as well talk to you.

What's a nice girl like you
doing with a face like that?

———•·•———

With a little surgery,
you wouldn't be half bad.

———•·•———

Beauty is only a light switch away.

———•·•———

You're ugly, but you intrigue me.

Do Nice Guys Neg?

One of the world's great pickup artists, Mystery (AKA Erik Von Markovik) has pioneered a controversial practice known as *negging*, making a "subtle-yet-negative statement that puts a target off-guard and makes her question her own value." According to Mystery, the response to a successful neg is laughter, but it also increases a woman's susceptibility to advances. While anecdotal evidence suggests negging works, proceed with caution.

ALL ABOUT ME

When you're obviously God's gift

A BIG EGO MEANS A LOT OF CON-
fidence, and confidence is a very
seductive trait. With these lines,
you can communicate that self-
assurance to your target. Whether
you're honestly assessing your
assets or exaggerating them for
effect, others will respect your
poise and certainty. People are
attracted to a healthy dose of
self-love, so go ahead and brag.

Take Wing

Playing wingman is a time-honored tradition. The newest twist, however, is the wingwoman, a good-looking gal pal recruited (or paid—through dedicated wingwomen services, no less) by a guy to help break the ice, put prospective pickups at ease, *and* demonstrate the guy's attractiveness. There's no reason why women shouldn't utilize the opposite-sex wingperson as well—nothing inspires male attention like a little competition.

To best harness this technique, get into the mindset before unleashing your pickup line. You are the greatest, and meeting you will make someone's day. Whether you're flaunting your good looks, bank account, or sexual prowess, by publicizing your strengths you will be giving your intended a little taste of what's in store.

Determine your approach to maximize your endowments and minimize your shortcomings. If your looks fall a little short, deflect attention to your bedroom skills or your big fat wallet. If you're broke, make note of your artistic integrity or smooth moves.

If all else fails, try another direction—woe is you. Capitalize on your misfortune and embody the opposite of the big ego by telling your sad, sad tale. Let sympathy and pity do the heavy lifting. If you underscore stories of your pathetic life with lost-puppy-dog eyes, who will be able to resist?

Above all, open and close with the biggest self-confidence booster around, positive thinking: assume you are desired and it will be so.

But Enough About You

As a matter of fact, I *am*
God's gift to women!

Did you hear the latest health
report? You need to up your
intake of Vitamin Me.

Congratulations! We just held
a secret lottery, and the grand
prize is a night with me.

Do you have a name,
or can I call you mine?

My name is Justin . . .
just incredible.

My name is Doug. That's
"God" spelled backward,
with a little bit of *U* in it.

When God was creating Earth,
he said, "Let there be perfection,"
and then there was me.

———————

If somebody were to write
your biography, the climax
would be meeting me.

———————

People are in your life for a reason, a
season, or a lifetime, and baby, when it
comes to me, two out of three ain't bad.

———————

Not many guys are special enough
to get me to talk to them.

———————

First buy me a drink, and then we'll talk.

———————

You know what I like
about you? My arms.

———————

This is your lucky day—
I just happen to be single.

You already have a *boy*friend? Well, when
you want a *man*friend, come see me.

You just may be good enough
to bear my children.

Okay, I'm here! What's
your second wish?

Hi, I'm Mr. Right. Someone
said you were looking for me.

Real men don't need pickup lines.

I'm a Sexy Beast

Damn! And I thought
I was good-looking!

I know it's dark, but trust me,
I'm the hottest one here.

Fortunately for you, I'm
more than just eye candy.

———•·•———

Must you stare?

———•·•———

They say a picture is worth a thousand
words, but mine is insured for a million.

———•·•———

You know, I need a license
to carry these guns.

Focus Your Braggadocio

If you're going to discuss yourself in a positive
light, you may as well zoom in on the qualities
that your targets are seeking, such as the
following top three attractors, according to an
AOL-Match.com survey.

Men
1. Physical appear-
   ance and body
2. Beautiful face
   and eyes
3. Sense of humor

Women
1. Sense of humor
2. Physical appear-
   ance and body
3. Caring and
   sensitivity

Why don't you drop the zero
and get with a hero?

———◆———

Are you really as beautiful
as you seem, or do you just
remind me of myself?

———◆———

You know, when the light hits your
eyes from this angle, I can see myself.

———◆———

You're definitely a 9, but you'd be a
perfect 10 if you were with me.

———◆———

Don't hate me because I'm
beautiful. Instead, love me
because I'll reflect well on you.

———◆———

I thought I'd come over before you and
your friends start fighting over me.

———◆———

Do you believe in love at first
sight, or should I walk by again?

You seem to have the confidence to be with someone as good-looking as me.

———•·•———

Who wouldn't want these genes?

I'm Hella Rich

I hate to use another lame pickup line, but who needs class when you got cash?

———•·•———

Someone as beautiful as you deserves someone as rich as me.

———•·•———

I'm rich, you're beautiful. What more do we need?

———•·•———

Do you have change for a ten-thousand-dollar bill?

———•·•———

Do you want my phone number, or would you just like to google it?

Tip: The Subtle Boast

Some pickup targets will be put off by overt crowing, so you'll want to learn some tricks to imply your assets without coming off as a total peacock. The restrained approach requires a deft, roundabout touch. Rather than saying you went to Yale, reminisce about a favorite New Haven haunt. Offhandedly mention that you need a receipt for your manager or broker. Talk about the quality of the light in Paris. The stealthy impression will be priceless.

Have you ever made out in the back seat of a Ferrari?

My yacht's only forty feet long, but I've got a hell of a personality.

Have you ever made love on a pile of money?

Your eyes are the exact same
color as my Bentley.

I want a man who
can see past my obscene
wealth to the *real* me.

I don't look like much, but wait
until you see my bank account.

If it doesn't work out between
us, you'll walk away with the
summerhouse and half of my assets.

Does money run in your family?
Well, it does in mine.

My chef makes the best
breakfast you've ever tasted.

My money can't make me
happy, but you can.

You'd make a hell of a trophy wife.

———•◦•———

You know, I'm actually
not that tall. I'm just
sitting on my wallet.

———•◦•———

I can't take you to heaven,
but my private helicopter
can get you close.

———•◦•———

Let's blow this joint and make love
in one of my five mansions.

———•◦•———

Who's your daddy?

I Got Moves

Champagne can tickle your
throat, and so can I.

———•◦•———

I do calisthenics every day—
with my tongue.

How would you like never to
have to fake it again?

———•—•———

I'm not Fred Flintstone,
but I'll make your bed rock.

———•—•———

It's not the size of the boat,
it's the motion in the ocean.

———•—•———

I grind so fine,
they call me coffee.

———•—•———

You know how they say
skin is the largest organ?
Not in my case.

———•—•———

I come with references.

———•—•———

I love bananas.

———•—•———

Don't you recognize me from
your wildest dreams?

You don't know me, but you've been
shouting my name for years.

———•———

I took a class at the Learning Annex.

———•———

Hey, just watch how I dance.

———•———

I can do the splits—
both ways.

———•———

When they tested Viagra,
I was the control group.

———•———

I'm a gynecologist, so I really know
my way around down there.

———•———

If you want to know what
I'm like in bed, go have a look
on the bathroom wall.

———•———

I'm so good, I get paid for it.

Woe Is Me

I'm shipping out tomorrow to a combat zone. I could die.

———•◦•———

I just got dumped. Would you boost my self-esteem?

———•◦•———

I promised my therapist I would at least *try* to ask someone out.

Cultivating the Inner Coach

Confidence is by far one of the most sexually attractive traits. The negative messages we replay in our heads have been scientifically shown to subliminally communicate to others and derail positive interactions, so you should go into every pickup situation reciting your own positive mantra (e.g., "I am the hottest person here tonight" or "I have stellar verbal skills"). Should you accidentally say it out loud, all the better.

I have to turn myself in
tomorrow, and I could get life.

It's not contagious.

The great thing about
being so short and fat is
I overcompensate in other ways.

Do you hear that? It's my
biological clock ticking.

The injury didn't affect my
performance abilities, but it did
make it harder to pick up women.

A close relative died
today, and I could really
use the support.

My husband doesn't
understand me.

My wife doesn't
understand me.

———◆———

I don't understand me.

———◆———

You'd be amazed how
many people are turned
off by my condition.

———◆———

I lost my job today.
Please don't make me deal
with another rejection.

———◆———

I lost the lottery today.
Please buy me a drink.

———◆———

Be unique and different—
just say yes.

———◆———

I'll pay you.

CONTEXT-
SPECIFIC

When location counts

IF YOU'RE IN THE SAME PLACE,
you've already got something in
common—location, location, location! Drawing on shared interests, from love of sun and sand
to contempt for laundry day, is
one of the best ways to initiate an
encounter and ensure subsequent
meetings in new places of interest.

Don't let any opportunity for a
pickup pass you by. Even the most

The Grand Gesture

Life moves fast. If you miss your opportunity to use a pickup line, try the grand gesture. In 2007, Patrick Moberg saw the woman of his dreams on a New York subway—but lost her in a crowd. Moberg drew a picture of the woman and posted it online with a plea for help. Within two days, he had been connected to his fantasy babe. If a grand gesture comes to fruition, just think of the stories you'll be able to tell your grandchildren!

mundane activities are laced with the chance to meet and greet. Whether standing in line for your morning coffee, photocopying office memos, or taking it to another level on the Stairmaster, look around— your dream date (or just tonight's date) could be right next to you. And if he or she is, you'll want to be prepared with the right words.

Every location can inspire its own
made-to-order lines simply by
incorporating the vocabulary of the
setting, offering to help with the
place-specific activity, or remarking
on goings-on. This chapter pro-
vides come-ons for various environ-
ments, from the beach to the café,
from the retirement home to the
yoga class. After studying these
lines, you'll be able to improvise
at any locale by utilizing or adapt-
ing the accoutrements at hand.

Location-specific overtures go
beyond the standard pickup and tip
into the arena of small talk. When
you make a clever, contextualized
comment, it seems improvised and
off-the-cuff rather than calculated
or smarmy. And when you appear
witty, natural, and spontaneous,
you'll be a magnet for attraction!

Beach

I think you missed a spot.

———•—•———

You're the hottest
thing since sunburn.

———•—•———

Want to jump in the
ocean with me? 'Cause
you've got me on fire.

———•—•———

Can I borrow your sunglasses?
Your beauty is blinding me.

———•—•———

I'd love to see you in a Speedo.

———•—•———

Excuse me—do you happen to
like long walks along the beach?

———•—•———

It's bodies like yours
that keep the dream of
nude beaches alive.

Come quick—my sand
castle needs a queen!

———•◦•———

Let's make crazy tan lines together.

Café

I like my coffee like I like my
men: hot, tall, and strong.

———•◦•———

You're sweeter than a decaffeinated
skim mocha with no whip.

———•◦•———

With you around, I don't
need sugar in my coffee.

———•◦•———

Do you like it steamy?
Creamy? Or both?

———•◦•———

Excuse me—are you reading? Your
lips aren't moving, so I wasn't
sure. You must be *really* smart.

I can't finish my pastry.
Would you like a bite?

———•———

I get horny when I'm caffeinated.

———•———

Is this seat taken?

Grocery Store

You better get out of that
express lane, 'cause you're all
that *and* a bag of chips.

———•———

I've got some meat here that's
"best if used by tonight."

———•———

What a coincidence!
You've got butter in your
cart, and I've got a copy of
Last Tango in Paris at home!

———•———

Let me guess from the contents
of your cart—you're single.

You're shopping for frozen,
but I can offer homemade.

———•◦•———

The way you squeezed
those melons, I could
tell we'd get along.

———•◦•———

How 'bout them apples?

The Most Unlikely Places

According to the *Los Angeles Times*, Stan Rosenfield was in the hospital, about to undergo a colonoscopy, when he noticed an anxious, attractive woman on the gurney next to his. He chatted her up and learned that she was nervous about having the same procedure. After reassuring her, he got her phone number and later took her to dinner. The moral of the story? No place (and no outfit—hospital gowns?) is off-limits for a pickup.

Gym

You look like you could kick some ass.

———◆———

Wanna come over?
You're already sweaty.

———◆———

I could use an extra workout tonight.

———◆———

When God invented Lycra,
he was thinking about you.

———◆———

I can tell you've got great stamina.

———◆———

You know, there are other
ways to release tension.

———◆———

What do you say we trade iPods
and see if we're compatible?

———◆———

Would you spot me?

Laundromat

Oh, no, I forgot detergent!

———•+•———

The whites go in with the
red socks, right?

———•+•———

Does that stain have a story?

———•+•———

It's the spin cycle—my favorite.

———•+•———

So . . . you bleach?

———•+•———

Is this thong yours?
I found it in the dryer.

———•+•———

You must use a ton of
fabric softener, because your
skin is smooth as silk.

———•+•———

Let's make our clothes
dirty all over again.

Come-On Contract

Thinking about picking up someone at work? You may first want to sign the flirting version of a prenup, the "consensual relationship agreement," AKA the love contract. Originated by the prominent employment law firm Littler Mendelson, the document, signed by coworkers about to embark on an affair, proclaims that both parties are entering into the relationship consensually, protecting everybody involved from future harassment charges.

Office

I'd really like to
interface your paradigm.

———◆———

Baby, I've got bandwidth to spare.

———◆———

Let's implement a
strategic initiative.

You have no idea what my
core competency is.

————•-•-•————

My value-added is my corner
office and a key to the executive
washroom. What's yours?

————•-•-•————

You've been top-of-mind lately.

————•-•-•————

I'd like to proactively
pursue a merger with you.

————•-•-•————

Let's make sure we're on the same
page—I'd love to see you after work.

————•-•-•————

You and me—synergy.

Places of Worship

WWJD? Tell you to go out with me.

————•-•-•————

I had a revelation about you.

Could we pray together sometime?

———•◦•———

With those muscles, you could
lug any size Torah around.

———•◦•———

Seriously, you're beautiful, but
it's your soul I'm interested in.

———•◦•———

Is it a sin that you stole my heart?

———•◦•———

Is that a Qur'an in your pocket,
or are you just glad to see me?

———•◦•———

God gave us these urges.
Who are we to deny them?

———•◦•———

How would you like a sneak
preview of heaven?

———•◦•———

You're going to send me
right to confession.

I predicted David over Goliath.

You know Jesus?
Hey, me too!

Retirement Home

Have you ever made love on
a motorized scooter?

I didn't know parts of me still
worked until I saw you.

I've got prescriptions that'll
blow your mind.

You'd be amazed what I can
do without my dentures.

You make the feeling come
back in my legs.

If it weren't for my trick knee,
I'd sweep you right off your feet.

———•———

My memory isn't what it used
to be. Have we met before?

———•———

You make me feel
seventy again.

School

I'm glad I have a library
card because I really like
checking you out.

———•———

You're by far my favorite subject.

———•———

How'd you like to earn
some extra credit?

———•———

I can teach you things you
won't find in any book.

The teacher thought I was cheating
because I can't take my eyes off you.

———————

I'm majoring in English and
I still can't describe your beauty.

———————

You may not be that smart,
but your body's an A-plus.

———————

Your dorm room or mine?

GPS for Singles

MoSoSo stands for mobile social software,
applications that reveal your location to
friends, friends-of-friends, or other subscrib-
ers with similar interests (e.g., singles) with
automated messages to their cell phones. You
are also notified of their proximity. Popular
with college students, MoSoSo allows people
to find like-minded early-adopters in their
vicinity. What better way to stage a pickup
wherever you happen to find yourself?

Wedding

Hey—we're both all dressed
up *with* a place to go.

———•◆•———

I'd buy you a drink, but they're free.

———•◆•———

You know, you're really not
supposed to outshine the bride.

———•◆•———

You know, I am the best
man for a reason.

———•◆•———

Wouldn't we look cute on
a wedding cake together?

———•◆•———

We both chose the chicken!
It must be fate.

———•◆•———

I bet you're going to catch the bouquet.

———•◆•———

I like your cummerbund.

Yoga

I see that you're bendy.

———•—•———

Do you need help
with your inversion?

———•—•———

God, how do you do that?

———•—•———

I sure do like your downward dog.

———•—•———

It's a shame you don't walk around
in leotards all day long.

———•—•———

Before coming to this class,
I specialized in tantric.

———•—•———

Let's practice our
breathwork together.

———•—•———

I met Sting once.

PEOPLE-SPECIFIC

When tailoring your line to their role

COMPLEMENTARY TO THE PLACE-specific pickup line is the person- or role-specific come-on. You might not know his name, but you know what he does—and he does it well. Referencing someone's livelihood is a classic approach and a great icebreaker. Whether your interaction is a one-time occurrence or you see someone on a day-to-day basis, talking with

Effective Flirting

By practicing a few easy techniques, you'll be able to attract all types of hotties. First, when he's talking, listen and pay attention; don't be thinking of what *you* are going to say next. Then, mimic and rephrase: mirror his body language and verbal style, restating and agreeing with his comments. Repeat his name whenever possible. Finally, ask questions: make him feel like the center of your universe. The most important tip? Smile.

your target about her profession and skills will open the door.

As with location-specific pickups, these lines earn points for focus and creativity. You can pick up on career-related interests and play to your crush's expertise. Most likely he already knows a little— or a lot—about you, too: what you like to drink, how much you tip, where you live, or, in the case of a therapist, your deep inner thoughts. This can generate appeal or aversion, so play your cards carefully.

In addition to peppering your come-ons with vocational lingo, you'll want to consider unique approaches to suit individual professions. A hot bartender probably hears a lot of lines, so make yours intriguing. For a customer service rep, use a sultry tone for delivery. A doctor has seen it all, so add a little mystery. And for the therapist, go for the breakthrough.

Your goal, of course, is to make your way into a hard-working person's heart via their chosen livelihood. Best of all, unlike with many pickups, you can be sure in these instances that your future paramour is employed.

Bartender

What time do you
get off, and how?

———•·•———

If you get any closer,
I'll need more ice.

———•·•———

I've got great problems. Do you
want to hear about them?

———•·•———

I like it shaken, not stirred,
because you shake so well.

———•·•———

You're strictly top-shelf.

———•·•———

Just think of it
as a really big tip.

———•·•———

What's your day job?

Customer Service Rep

Ooh, does that accent
mean you're in India?

———

No, thank you for *taking* my call.

———

I bet you look really
sexy in a headset.

———

Have you considered doing
voice-over work?

———

I can't imagine you process
returns for just anybody.

———

Does it make you hot that this
call might be recorded?

———

I've always wanted someone
with an 800 number.

Doctor

I'd drop my pants for you any day.

———•••———

You really raise my blood pressure.

———•••———

I'm an organ donor—need anything?

———•••———

Would you prefer my gown
open in the front or back?

———•••———

I'm not afraid of needles, but I
prefer being otherwise penetrated.

———•••———

I feel like you can really see inside
me, and it's not just the X-rays.

———•••———

You palpate so gently.

———•••———

With a bedside manner like that,
I can't imagine how anybody
ever lets you out of bed.

Gardener

Let's give "mow, blow, and go" a whole new meaning.

Would you like another hedge to trim?

Other men may bring me flowers, but you tend them.

Tip: Props for Props

Utilizing props can really help to break the ice. Depending on your quarry's occupation, use something in the environment to start a conversation. Ask your doctor for her stethoscope and listen to *her* heartbeat. Take the cherry from your drink and tell your bartender you can tie its stem in a knot without using your hands. Grab a broom and whisk your janitor off his feet. Having something tangible to focus on will immediately form a bond between you.

Is it hard to handle a hose that big?

So what made you decide to
specialize in the agricultural field?

When I think of what your hands
do to my plants, I can only imagine
what they could do to me.

I wouldn't mind being fertilized.

Geek

You turn my software into hardware.

What's a maiden like you doing
in a dungeon like this?

Your graphics rival Doom 3.

You may be a geek by day, but I bet
you're a sex machine by night!

I'd like to instantiate your objects,
and access their member variables.

———•·•———

I hope you don't have a firewall, because
I want to access all your ports.

———•·•———

I'll input if you'll output.

Maintenance Person

I feel so close to you now that
you've plunged my toilet.

———•·•———

My hinge could use a little grease.

———•·•———

That tool belt really brings
out the green in your eyes.

———•·•———

Would you like to nail me?

———•·•———

Why do you prefer to screw?

71

UPS or FedEx?

According to the *Wall Street Journal*, "brown-collar fantasies" are rampant. Now that FedEx is offering ground service, however, the intimacy has extended to wearers of the blue, and a "Whose is sexier?" uniform rivalry has arisen among the carriers themselves. Both services have resulted in countless dates and even a few customer-carrier marriages. Still, with its phone number, 1-800-PICK-UPS, UPS will always be the top inspiration for pickup artists.

Can you hammer all day long?

My, you're handy.

Package Carrier

Wow, that's quite a package.

I could think of something *else*
I'd like from you instead.

I see where to sign my name, but
where can I leave my number?

———◆———

This box may have
been sent by ground, but
you're strictly overnight.

———◆———

Wow, you sure do deliver.

———◆———

They didn't mention I'd get
such special handling.

———◆———

You already know where I live.
Do you have any other questions?

Police Officer

You didn't just pull me over
for a citation, right?

———◆———

You've got sirens, I *am*
a siren—it's perfect!

What do you do with
those handcuffs when
you're not working?

—◆—

I bet you're a top-notch shooter.

—◆—

I love a man in a uniform—
but I like it even better when
he's out of his uniform.

—◆—

Want to run me
through your system?

—◆—

My driver's license doesn't do
my nude pictures justice.

Store Clerk

Did you major in retail services?

—◆—

Was "Leave a penny, take
a penny" your idea?

Let's do something for
the hidden camera!

I know you're working the late
shift, but would you consider
pulling a double—at my house?

Can you recommend
a good malt liquor?

If I were to shoplift,
what would you do to me?

You really fill out that smock.

Therapist

Enough about me—
what is it that relaxes *you*?

I think I could have a breakthrough
if you sat on the couch with me.

How do I really feel? Soft and silky.

———•·•———

You remind me of my first
memory of sex.

———•·•———

You understand me so much
better than my wife does.

———•·•———

How can you truly know me without
coming over to my house for drinks?

———•·•———

One word—oedipal.

Waiter

The menu looks good. Are you on it?

———•·•———

It's only fair: you're serving me
dinner, I'll cook you breakfast.

———•·•———

Oh, I like it hot. Hot and spicy.

Don't you have any *other* condiments?

———

Is there anything that's
not on the menu?

———

I'd like to try something exotic.
What do you recommend?

———

I'll have the cheese balls.

Vocational Sexiness

According to an annual Salary.com survey,
the ten sexiest professions for 2008 were
firefighter (obviously number one), personal
trainer, CEO, bartender, nurse, photographer,
pilot, surgeon, cowboy, and soldier. The list
changes significantly from year to year, so
be sure to stay up to date. When approach-
ing these individuals, you'll want to use your
A-game. Or, to increase your odds, consider a
career change and let others hit on you!

COITUS SEEKING

When getting down to business

LET'S BE HONEST—A PICKUP OR
a come-on is, at its most basic, an
invitation for sex. Whether you
want to park the pink Cadillac,
make the beast with two backs,
or bump uglies, sex is what it's
all about. These lines get right to
the point, from simply suggestive to indisputably disgusting.

Although the majority of lines in
this book are meant to swing either

Safe Is Sexy

When you're out on the town looking for Mr. or Ms. Right Now, be prepared. The Centers for Disease Control estimates that 19 million new STD infections occur each year. Carry unexpired condoms and be prepared to prove your HIV status. While healthy protocols and disease-free status will help you once you've attracted a potential partner, avoid incorporating them into your pickups; "Hey, baby, the clinic says I'm clean now" is generally a loser.

way, this chapter includes a special section of sex-seeking phrases for women to men—basically, "Hi" will suffice. No matter what gender you're attracting, however, it will most likely take more than that.

Before blurting out your line, you'll want to consider what your desired outcome is. Sex, of course, but are you hoping for a second date? Or is this a one-night-only opportunity? Also, you'll need to weigh the potential reaction of your prospective bedmate. Will you get slapped, will he need to be coaxed into bed, or will he jump into your lap before you even open your mouth?

Use the sections in this chapter according to your intuition about and intentions for the recipient: suggestive (lines you could express in front of others or for sweet-talking foreplay), overt (no bones about it), and kinda nasty (kinda nasty).

Whichever approach you take, when you can't contain yourself any longer, remember that sex is a basic instinct, squelch your shame, say it like it is, and clear the table, because sometimes the extremely direct approach can be so startling as to be extremely effective.

Women to Men

Hi.

———•———

Hello.

———•———

Good morning.

———•———

Nice to meet you.

———•———

Thank you.

———•———

You're welcome.

———•———

Excuse me.

———•———

Pardon me.

———•———

Could you move your cart?

Which way is the ladies' room?

———•—•———

Is this the end of the line?

———•—•———

Third floor, please.

———•—•———

Are you using that chair?

———•—•———

Asshole!

Suggestive

Want to come up and see my etchings?

———•—•———

Global warming.
Need I say more?

———•—•———

I know a great way to kill ten minutes.

———•—•———

I know a great way to
commune with God.

Guess what I saw on Animal
Planet the other night?

Do you mind if I end this
sentence in a proposition?

You know, it's not premarital sex
unless you plan on getting married.

Nice dress. Can I talk you out of it?

I could fall madly in bed with you.

Hi, I'm foreign. I've got Russian
hands and Roman fingers.

You know how some men buy
really expensive cars to make
up for certain shortages?
Well, I don't even own a car.

You deserve a good spanking.

I spent over a grand on Viagra
today only to see you and realize
I don't need it after all.

———•◦•———

Screw me if I'm wrong,
but haven't we met before?

———•◦•———

That jewelry would look
great on my nightstand.

Body Language: Yours

Experts say body language communicates
more than half of your message, so be aware!
Skillful body language can subconsciously sug-
gest compatibility to your target. Take your
hands out of your pockets. Synchronize your
movements with hers. Place an item in her
personal space. Lean back when you converse
to indicate power and confidence. Keep your
hands still, not fidgety. Or, if you're not into
subtle, you can always lean in for a first kiss.

When I think of you it's X-rated.

You bring a whole new meaning
to the word "edible."

I'm easy. Are you?

Overt

I just learned the most acrobatic
new sexual technique. Would
you like to try it?

If you sleep with me,
I'll leave you alone.

Have sex with me and
I'll make you a star.

Excuse me. I'm from the FBI—the Fine
Body Investigators—and I'm going to
have to ask you to assume the position.

You'd look great reflected on my ceiling.

———•—•———

My bed is broken. Can I sleep in yours?

———•—•———

Help the homeless—
take me home with you.

———•—•———

Should I call you in the
morning or nudge you?

———•—•———

You won't have to wait for my call
tomorrow if you sleep over.

———•—•———

Are you a virgin? No? Prove it!

———•—•———

Come over here and get a taste
of America's Most Wanted.

———•—•———

Do you know what'd look
good on you? Me.

Body Language: Theirs

When trying to determine whether someone is interested, look for these signals. Does she square off to face you? Look at your mouth a lot? Preen or adjust clothing, jewelry, or hair? Have raised eyebrows? Expose palms or wrists to you? Lean toward you when you speak? Have dilated pupils? Touch you during conversation? If you're lucky enough to catch a few of these physical clues, know that you're on the right track, headed for the station.

Excuse me. Where does the line start to get in your pants?

———•◦•———

Let's have a party and invite your pants to come on down.

———•◦•———

I'm new to this country, and you're the prettiest sight I've seen. I'd like to arrange a guided tour of your body.

You've been a bad, bad boy.
Now go to my room!

I may be easy, but it looks
like you're hard.

Do you sleep on your stomach? Can I?

I'll tell you my favorite sexual
positions if you'll tell me yours.

Let's go to my place and do the things
that I'll tell my friends we did anyway.

I bet it's been a long time
since you've been laid.

You look like you could
use a one-night stand.

Let's make out so I can see if you
taste as good as you look.

You're drunk. I'm drunk.
Let's screw.

Let's bypass all the bullshit
and get naked.

Do you know the difference
between sex and conversation?
You don't? Do you want to
go upstairs and talk?

Don't worry, I won't ask you
to screw. I'm British—we're
not like that. Wanna shag?

I'm looking for treasure.
Can I check your chest?

I'd like to name a multiple
orgasm after you.

Lie down. I think I love you.

COITUS SEEKING

Hi. Do you have any STDs
I should know about before
we introduce ourselves?

———•—•———

I'd love to swap fluids with you.

———•—•———

I work at a condom
factory. Want to help me
test my product?

———•—•———

Are you into threesomes?

———•—•———

That outfit is really ugly. You
should take it off immediately.

———•—•———

Your daddy must play the trumpet,
because he sure made me horny!

———•—•———

I'm horny.

———•—•———

Enough conversation.
Let's do it.

Kinda Nasty

You may have heard about me—
I specialize in cunnilingus.

Would you like to set down
on my Brazilian? Some people
call it a landing strip.

Can I walk through your bushes
and climb your mountains?

My hands are cold. Can I warm
them in your heaving breasts?

My hands are cold. Can I stick
them down your pants?

Are you as easy as you look?

Do you have any Benadryl? Every
time I look at you I have swelling.

I've got the ship, you've got the harbor—
what say we tie up for the night?

I'm a dog, and I need to bury my bone.

I want to melt in your mouth,
not in your hand.

Are you a sergeant? 'Cause you make
my privates stand up straight.

Movies, Between Your Legs

The next time you're on the prowl, have some off-the-script fun with this witty game: take any movie title and add "between my legs" for a marquee-worthy tagline. As with appending the words "in bed" to fortune-cookie fortunes ("You will soon achieve success . . . in bed!"), this little trick is a guaranteed icebreaker. "It's *Toy Story* . . . between my legs!" "It's *Superman Returns* . . . between my legs!" The opportunities—and the fun—are endless.

Do you know the difference between a hamburger and a blow job? You don't? Would you like to do lunch?

———•—•———

Do you like whales? Well, I have a humpback at my place.

———•—•———

Hey baby, let's play house—you can be the door, and I'll slam you!

———•—•———

How do you like your eggs in the morning? Fertilized?

———•—•———

I'm Irish. Do you have any Irish in you? Would you like some?

———•—•———

Do you want to see why the girls call me "tripod"?

———•—•———

That shirt's very becoming on you. If I were on you, I'd be coming, too.

The word of the day is "legs." Let's head
back to your place and spread the word.

———•—•———

My, that's a nice set of legs.
What time do they open?

———•—•———

If I flip a coin, what do you reckon
my chances are of getting head?

———•—•———

I bet you could suck Lincoln's
head off a penny.

———•—•———

Are those lumberjack pants you're
wearing? They're giving me wood.

———•—•———

There are 265 bones in the human
body. How would you like one more?

———•—•———

There are a lot of fish in the sea, but
you're the only one I'd like to mount.

———•—•———

Wasn't I supposed to eat you somewhere?

FAMOUS
FLIRTATIONS

When wits try to mate

HAVE YOU EVER IMAGINED HOW great your pickup lines could be if they were written by Hollywood screenwriters, literary giants, television scribes, or rock stars? To provide you with come-on inspiration, this chapter presents a panoply of some of the best-loved and most clever pickup lines ever crafted.

The functionality of these lines doesn't end at inspiration—you

Come-On Lingo

Pickups, flirting, and dating have spawned their own vocabulary. When you *hyperdate*, you indiscriminately set up numerous dates, usually through an online service. *Intellidating*, however, means you carefully choose cultured dating destinations like museums or lectures. Perhaps there, you will meet a *retrosexual* (one with traditional sexual preferences). After any date, hope for a *bangover* (exhaustion due to sexual exertion; also *sexhaustion*).

can actually use them. You could choose to go the safe route (citing your source then discussing its provenance, i.e., where you were when you saw the movie, read the book, heard the song). Depending on the line, it could make you sound literate, intelligent, and cultured, or you could come off as a pop-culture junkie. If you feel you can get away with it, you could also try taking credit for the line as your own, sounding as smooth and as suave as the original creators did.

Pickups and come-ons have been around since the beginning of time—otherwise, how would the population have replaced itself? While many of the best no doubt went unrecorded (how many times do *you* stop to write down your best material?), there have been literary and musical types who've taken the time to craft verbal moves— whether for themselves or for fictional characters—to perfection.

By now you're a pro at the pickup game. Once you're ready to go off-script, it'll be no surprise if your sweet-talking savvy makes its way into the next version of this book.

Film

"You know, when you blow out the match, it's an invitation to kiss you."
—John Gilbert, *Flesh and the Devil*, 1926

"You're a swell dish. I think I'm gonna go for you." —James Cagney, *The Public Enemy*, 1931

"I'd like to run barefoot through your hair." —Franchot Tone, *Bombshell*, 1933

"You're so beautiful, it makes me want to gag." —Jimmy Stewart, *You Can't Take It with You*, 1938

"We're going to know each other eventually, why not now?" —Humphrey Bogart, *Across the Pacific*, 1942

"Was that cannon fire, or is it my heart pounding?" —Ingrid Bergman, *Casablanca*, 1942

"Everything wrong with you, I like."
—Van Johnson, *A Guy Named Joe*, 1944

———•◦•———

"Give me a kiss or I'll sock
you." —John Garfield, *The
Postman Always Rings Twice*, 1946

———•◦•———

"I was bored to death.
I hadn't seen one attractive woman
on this ship since we left. Now, isn't
that terrible? I was alarmed. I said
to myself, 'Don't beautiful women
travel anymore?' And then I saw you,
and I was saved—I hope." —Cary
Grant, *An Affair to Remember*, 1957

———•◦•———

"You know what's wrong with
you? Nothing." —Audrey
Hepburn, *Charade*, 1963

———•◦•———

"Let me try and enlarge your
vocabulary." —Roger Moore,
The Spy Who Loved Me, 1977

"I was born to love you. I was born to lick your face. I was born to rub you, but you were born to rub me first. What do you say we take this out on the patio?"
—Chevy Chase, *Caddyshack*, 1980

"What's happenin', hot stuff?" —Gedde Watanabe, *Sixteen Candles*, 1984

"Have you ever done it in an elevator?" —Glenn Close, *Fatal Attraction*, 1987

"What I'm saying is—and this is not a come-on in any way, shape or form—is that men and women can't be friends because the sex part always gets in the way." —Billy Crystal, *When Harry Met Sally*, 1989

"I am looking for a 'dare to be great' situation." —John Cusack, *Say Anything*, 1989

"I may be the outlaw, but you're the one stealin' my heart." —Brad Pitt, *Thelma and Louise*, 1991

"Swoon. I'll catch you." —Ralph Fiennes, *The English Patient*, 1996

"Do I make you horny, baby, yeah, do I?" —Mike Myers, *Austin Powers: International Man of Mystery*, 1997

Meeting Cute

Meet-cute is movie lingo for a scene in which two lovers meet in an unlikely and comic way. For example, in *Singin' in the Rain*, Gene Kelly plays a movie star who falls into driver Debbie Reynolds's convertible while escaping from fans. Meet-cute scenarios often involve spilling, fender-benders, saved lives, mistaken identities, and lost gloves. Endeavor to meet-cute with an object of your desire and at the very least you'll have a good story to tell.

"You make me want to be a better man."
—Jack Nicholson, *As Good As It Gets*, 1997

"Can you keep a secret? I'm trying to organize a prison break. We have to first get out of this bar, then the hotel, then the city, and then the country. Are you in or you out?" —Bill Murray, *Lost in Translation*, 2003

Television

"I figure a girl like you has heard all the phony lines in the book . . . so one more isn't going to hurt . . . Walk with me. Talk with me." —Andy Kaufman, *Taxi*, c. 1978

"Hey lady, want to lick my mail?"
—Bruce Willis, *Moonlighting*, 1985

"You know, I'm the one responsible for those crop circles in England."
—Jerry Seinfeld, *Seinfeld*, 1990

"I like your butt . . . I mean your bike."
—Shannen Doherty, *90210*, 1990

⸻

"Hey baby, I noticed you noticing
me and I just wanted to put you on
notice that I noticed you too." —Will
Smith, *The Fresh Prince of Bel-Air*, 1990

⸻

"How *you* doin'?"
—Matt LeBlanc, *Friends*, 1994

⸻

"How about when the alert level goes
down, and the terrorists have been
caught, we can have some chamomile
tea and I'll tell you all my secrets?"
—Mary Lynn Rajskub, *24*, 2001

⸻

"Come and get me sailors."
—Kim Cattrall, *Sex in the City*, 2002

⸻

"Michael, you are quite the
cupid. You can stick an arrow in
my buttocks any time." —David
Cross, *Arrested Development*, 2003

Producers vs. Receptors

It takes two to joke—the comic and the laugher, AKA the producer and the receptor. A sense of humor is desirable by both men and women. According to a university study, however, passive-active gender stereotypes prevail when joking around: women choose men who *produce* humor 62 percent of the time, while men choose women who *appreciate* their humor 65 percent of the time. At least it's even; let's hope the other 35 percent are LOL.

Music

"I get no kick from champagne / Mere alcohol doesn't thrill me at all / So tell me why should it be true / That I get a kick out of you?" —Cole Porter, "I Get a Kick Out of You," 1934

"Why do birds suddenly appear / Every time you are near? / Just like me, they long to be / Close to you." —Burt Bacharach, "Close to You," 1963

"Hello, I love you / Won't you tell me your name? / Hello, I love you / Let me jump in your game." —The Doors, "Hello I Love You," 1968

———•·•———

"Well, I'm a steamroller baby / I'm bound to roll all over you." —James Taylor, "Steamroller," 1970

———•·•———

"Tonight's the night." —Rod Stewart, "Tonight's the Night," 1976

———•·•———

"If you like piña coladas / And getting caught in the rain." —Rupert Holmes, "Escape," 1979

———•·•———

"All I want is one night of glory / I don't even know your second name." —Elvis Costello, "Different Finger," 1981

———•·•———

"Why don't we get drunk and screw? / I just bought a waterbed filled up for me and you." —Jimmy Buffet, "Why Don't We Get Drunk," 1985

"Hike up your skirt a little bit more / and show the world to me." —Dave Matthews, "Crash Into Me," 1999

"Your body is a wonderland." —John Mayer, "Your Body Is a Wonderland," 2001

"All the other girls here are stars— you are the Northern Lights." —Josh Ritter, "Kathleen," 2003

"Cause you're the only song I want to hear / A melody softly soaring through my atmosphere." —Death Cab for Cutie, "Soul Meets Body," 2005

"I think it's special, what's behind your back? / So turn around and I'll pick up the slack." —Justin Timberlake, "Sexyback," 2006

Literature

"To blurt it out in a word— we want laying." —Aristophanes, *Lysistrata*, 411 BC

———————

"I wrong you not if I my thoughts reveal, / Saying how the beauty that your clothes conceal / Is like a spark that sets afire my heart. / I only ask that you then, for your part, / Will be a saddle and let me ride, / Just for this once." —François Rabelais, *Gargantua and Pantagruel*, 1534

———————

"Graze on my lips; and if these hills be dry, / Stray lower, where the pleasant fountains lie." —William Shakespeare, "Venus and Adonis," 1593

———————

"License my roving hands, and let them go, / Before, behind, between, above, below." —John Donne, "To His Mistress Going to Bed," c. 1595

"Was this the face that launched a thousand ships, / And burnt the topless towers of Ilium? / Sweet Helen, make me immortal with a kiss!" —Christopher Marlowe, *Doctor Faustus*, 1604

———•◦•———

"See my lips tremble, and my eyeballs roll / Suck my last breath, and catch my flying soul." —Alexander Pope, "Eloisa to Abelard," 1717

———•◦•———

"Do me the favour to deny me at once." —Benjamin Franklin, *Poor Richard's Almanack*, 1746

———•◦•———

"O for you, whoever you are, your correlative body! O it, more than all else, you delighting!" —Walt Whitman, *Leaves of Grass*, 1860

———•◦•———

"I want to do with you what spring does with cherry trees." —Pablo Neruda, "Every Day You Play," 1924

"i like, slowly stroking the, shocking
fuzz / of your electric fur, and
what-is-it comes / over parting flesh ..."
—e. e. cummings, "i like my body
when it is with your body," 1925

"But did thee feel the earth
move?" —Ernest Hemingway,
For Whom the Bell Tolls, 1940

The Real Casanova

The name synonymous with seduction, Casanova, is actually connected to a human being,
eighteenth-century Venetian adventurer, intel-
lect, author, and ladies' man Giovanni Giacomo
Casanova. His autobiography, *Story of My Life*,
details his numerous conquests (over one hun-
dred!) with the fairer sex—and more. Orgies,
threesomes, and voyeurism provide an authen-
tic look at the not-so-old-fashioned European
courting and mating customs of his age.

"*All those curves, and me with no brakes.*"